Advan

Fidelitoria is where poetry and sorcery waltz together. Candice Wuehle has a masterful lens on the veiled extraordinary of our world. Poetry reorients itself to epistle then back again, with a strength and direction I long for in every poet's work, "Frisk your own nature most ardently, adorn your edges with blood-bruises."

— **CAConrad**

Fidelitoria comprises nothing less than a deck of spells—spilling over with poems that seethe as they seek out whatever's beyond the limits of becoming. I can feel the warp of Alice Notley's necromancy, and perhaps the weft, too, of Hannah Weiner's clairvoyant visions. Yet Wuehle's poetics summon her own "zodiacal darkening"—both lucid and spooky—as she threads hex-like verses into a roiling hallucination. I haven't been this ecstatically disturbed by a collection of poetry since I was somebody else. Take this weird book with you where you're going. Or don't—and suffer. But you've been warned now, haven't you?

— **Joshua Marie Wilkinson**

Candice Wuehle's *Fidelitoria: fixed or fluxed* is a dynamic, enthralling collection whose electric live wire lines twitch and quake as all divinations do—animated with excess wisdom and ancient energies. These poems are searing, celebratory, and intimate; Wuehle uses poetry as a conduit between bewilderment and forecast, utterance and occult, trauma and pain song, archive and dirt. The spirits are here, and Wuehle warns "One thing you can't do / Is go back and draw the cards / In the time before." Let these poems serve as clues to our shared fate.

— **Caryl Pagel**

There is an irresistible melancholy of chaos living here, binding and unwinding like tree's leaves and seasonal diurnal gowns, not resisting a fluorescent medium of abundance and snow. Here the speaker travels through her own tongue to find herself over and over, in herbs, in aliens, in the quiet spectacular. In the banquet of tarot and bucolic poetry, where the lexical grass grows things such as prohilil and exnihil while the poet takes us through her undertone of lugubrious surrender. Timeless and elongated, with repetitive mantra that behave hypnotically like falling floral faunas, Candice Wuehle hopes, in this wild spellbinding of lexical restfulness, to achieve accretion of self through the oracular amnesia of self.

— **Vi Khi Nao**

FIDELITORIA
fixed or fluxed

Candice Wuehle

Cover Art by Mike Corrao

Paperback: 9781948687270

Printed in the United States of America

FIRST AMERICAN EDITION

9 8 7 6 5 4 3 2 1

Since misrecognition is inevitable, since the fantasmatic projection onto objects of desire

that

crack you open

and

give you back to yourself

in a way about which you might feel many ways will always happen in any circuit of reciprocity with the world,

why fight it?

—Lauren Berlant

Love can only consist in Failure.

—Alain Badiou

THE INDISCRETE TAROT

Another savory feeling in my mouth.
Starless solstice morning.
My dad
Drops me
At high school
And I'm alone
Again.
It's a snow day.
I don't care.
I go to the dark room.
I love the empty
Gymnasium, journalism room.
It's ok.
The janitor is also here and he has a set of keys and
Will give me access
If I find him.
I would have come
Anyway.
Me and dad don't listen to radio in the morning.
We don't check in.
It takes 15 years to stop dreaming of that day.
I have to divorce a whole man to make the dreams
Stop.
A whole one.
Women can learn to swim now.
I know that's a dumb thing to say/
I say dumb things.
I let people think I'm dumb.
Stay safe.
I love to be alone
And I love to live underwater.
I quit getting out of bed
To go to high school/
Dad said whatever.
Said/ end it early/

On to the next.

And I did.

Only I dreamed for 15 years.

A whole one.

In June I didn't wonder what happened/ But now I

Wonder what happened.

One thing you can't do

Is go back and draw the cards

In the time before

You knew how/

To draw.

Most people I draw for are the same

And draw the same:

Energy.

PAGE OF WANDS, CHARIOT, TOWER.

I see the TOWER all the time.

The rule of this poem

Is I can't give

Advice/ okay?

I want to say

/Like/ only watch *Diabolique* with another woman

You love in that one style

/You know/

You can image her bursting

Into gossamer scarves

You let her wash her blood

Y whites in your washer.

Well, I won't/

I'll exit and say me and best-friend

Watched *Bewitched* and never talked about

Why.

If I have to play Talent I still twitch

My nose.

Sincerely.

A little of the

h o t c h i t o t c h i b u n g a t o c h i is all

I've got.

Have you heard the phrase w o r k

Your m a g i c?

Breath holes.

Have you ever met a little boy
Who found out
Where babies
Come from in the worst way possible?
You can't usually betwitch one of those.
Bewitch.
I don't know myself or you   /
Very well.
Wind wind water fire.
I've been the President
Of the Hierophant Haters Club
This year.
I'm so sick
Of answers.
Remember the episode
Of *The Simpsons* when
Bart finds a pregnancy test
And also makes conceptual art?
I'm not bragging
But I'm an air sign. All I think about
Is my right relation to others.
Agamben says
Gossip is the personal truth
Which heals us.
Geramium neroli melissa sandalwood
Balm balm balm balm.
That episode was important.
Homer explained museums
Keep the art away
Because we hate it so much.

Gas chamber.

Has anyone ever asked you where your favorite

Place in the world is?
If a man asks you this
And THE WORLD
And THE 2 OF CUPS or
LOVERS
Appear in your spread
Some readers insist the rings of Saturn
As expressed in the bounded Capricornian WORLD
Will bind you to him.
It wasn't JANE AUSTEN AND THE
MASTURBATING GIRL it was
Something else where Eve Kosofsky Sedgwick says/
The best thing is to have no karma.
Good or bad. Saturn
Is the planet of invisible reins, retribution, it takes
28-30 years
To circle.
My favorite place was the black cylinder
Which sealed the light
So it never touched
The gelantized papers flopped over in
The 20 chemical baths.
I went there in the middle
Of that day
Just to stand
And breathe
In the dark.

///

It was THE WEATHER IN PROUST.

///

The roads are iced up.
The walls are made of tin.
It is like being undeveloped film.
I'm 17.
I'm a platinum blonde
Woman already.
I don't know what is going
To develop

But I do/
Really.
I do occult
Things in the cylinder.
I can see
Later/ later than now
I will have to cover mirrors.
Victoriana.
To experience hatred I go to auctions
And watch other women
Buy the guilt-edged objects
I want.
If I throw the cards right now/
All PENTACLES.
I was a mummy for Halloween
As a child/ all
Pins and tissue.
I always came undone
In an embarrassing way.
Now I sleep the same.
I tell men this
Like it's a warning
In the worst way possible
I say/
I sleep as if in a
Grave
Hands crossed
Across my chest.
Don't undo me.
Later
When spring comes
Best-friend starts calling
Before dawn
To tell me to
Remember to come
To high school, to spirit
Assembly.
I wonder

If Sedgwick wrote on the tarot.
If it breaks the affective sphere/
Ungoverns it gainfully/
If you can call affect the secretion
Which appropriates the future.
I'd like to really end this.
Let's just read Žižek's cards.
A sleeping draught/
Dream from late afternoon to dark.
Gold sparks come from
My solar plexus/
I get up.
Sage. Sage. Amethyst
On the edges of the deck:
WHAT COVERS HIM/
HIS OBSTACLES/
WHAT CROWNS HIM/
WHAT IS BENEATH HIM/
WHAT IS BEHIND HIM/
WHAT IS BEFORE HIM/
WHAT SIGNIFIES HIM/
WHAT SIGNIFIES HIS HOUSE/
HIS HOPES AND FEARS/
WHAT WILL COME/
THAT WHICH UNDERLIES ALL/
Energy and actuation/
No cups/
Inverted WANDS indicate bad faith.
Bad messages.
An entire element is missing.
DEATH can negate this/
Rosebush in aftertimes.
Underlying all is a teacher in a cathedral.
I make it
Through
One last spring and 18 days of autumn.
Everyone starts reciting the Auden that goes
The lights must never go out/
The music must always play.

The music must always play.
The music must always play.
The music must always play.
The music must always play.
I meet my husband
He asks me if I thought there was
But two or three pronunciations of the sound of my
Own Name?
I know that part is already
Over. I draw
The 3 OF SWORDS
And I draw the inverted EMPRESS.
I draw THE STAR/
Also. I draw

Everything the same
Again.

Adult best-friend texts
And asks if we're going
To meet our 2nd husbands at the bar tonight.
Only the FOOL
Can protect
From the DEVIL.
I thank
I thank
I thank
For my MB in Atlanta
For my PJR in Munich
For my SZ in Iowa City
For my ARB in New Orleans
For my RM in Philadelphia
For the cylinder
In which no must arose
Only
Absorptions of others
Echoes.

I'm not asking
For another snow day.
I'm saying

                                                    //////////
                                    It   is   okay
                                                    //////////

I myself am

              snow.

fixed

EARTH

X 1

There are only a few lives I think
you really could have done justice: deposed
dictator, abused queen. The night
our cat's body is cremated, he informs me
your response to the death reflected exactly
your mother's response to the death of
her husband. She lost all
composure. No,
no, no, no, no.

X 2

I never told you this.
It is Take Your Daughter to Work Day and I am
reading
a Sweet Valley Twins book when he taps my knee
and smiles,
points to the mouth
of the telephone to the coast
he is speaking to. Lifts a finger,
and lets it drop.
Then he rages. I laugh. He just flipped a
switch.

X 3

My hands are my slaves.
I protect and care for them
and in return they articulate my
will for me. What does Life mean

to you who with your hands do not even brush your
own hair?
My slaves work past exhaustion. Shake and weaken.
Send strong distress
to the bicep, to the cervical centers and still I
won't let them down. I once lived under a bar called
Ground X:
so much slapping.

X 4

In your last texts
you finally revel
in apology: CAND, LOVEU LUVON5 I MESSED UP.
You are the last one left who
knows how to make me open
my mouth to slavver nothing, who knows how to
hang.

X 5

You said I was the only woman you ever knew well
who was certain of her life
and I wondered if you meant to invent your own
monster
just to meet me. I implore
myself to imagine myself
as you were in the aisle of St. Mary's
the afternoon of your mother's funeral,
a sibling upholding you on either side.
If I knew you well I would tell you at the axis of my
life, there
is nothing. No hinge to come
unhinged, from. Instead
I imagine my first beautiful acting master

repeating these words:

<u>Your feet are on the floor</u>
<u>Your feet are on the floor</u>
<u>Your feet are on the floor</u>
and you in the impossible audience
a pile of unblown ash, odd
Last Ember.

AIR

Dear,

I talk less. Crowds happen and effort.

Luck makes the words

that cause listening. In the enclosure

I wait for anyone

to say in order

there are only two possibilities

and then I do it carefully.

In the nail care salon a woman from a state

I was once in told the television doctor

she was held in a cellar for ten years.

I put in the iPod and listened to Bruce

Springsteen and paid money and left. It is

fine to never experience murder

emotions. To have medium-feelings.

I am a thin woman.

I can slip out of many constructions,

I slipped out of that. In German I have long

been a machine only to now be

dead. How?

> Each completed digit
>
> creamed in bronze, lacquered
>
> decay
>
> and I think to say that when she saw
> her self styled in a mirror that
> woman thought her hair was
> beautiful. Fine. I too seek even now.

Dear,

It means not twisting your head

to look at your own back.

Dear,

I write to tell you I saw a Ouija run

in reverse.

10 9 8 7 6 5 4 3 2 1

Z Y X W V U T S R Q P O N M L K

I want idiot

words: learned helplessness. In the

clearing I tell the story of your last

telephone call.

You said violence. I was in a Borders; I said

I'm calling your twin. I am

unavailable to you.

I heard the Podcast: Dangerously

Unqualified Dating Disasters

which our friend now airs

with whom you stayed that day in the city

just today. My trapezius

has ached since the yes-yes device.

Dear,

Re-present your ear when slapped

and the slapping

is no longer an assaulting.

Dear,

Are you an asterisk

off the Word I used oftener once? Questions

like the above are why star wishes are

criminal. We cannot fall through

space.

I could step into a closet and close the door and
after three days and two hours and six minutes step
out and say that was three days and two hours and
six minutes. No

I couldn't.

I couldn't know how much longer

I've been here. I could if

space were a through-construct; if

when trapped

I did not relapse

and answer double.

Dear,

I try to feel formal

pressure but there isn't enough. I have a wig

which looks like my own hair I never

wear it out. Not anything could make me

send. Not all the

arms, not any soldier in this zone.

Anything could make me

Dear,

Anything could make me want

to add an end. Tend my life

through amendment.

I have avoided rule and offers and am still

prosecuted by subject

desire. The man who answers

his mail can call it

love. Never call one crushed

royalty. Easy descent

to indicative.

Dear,

Life is for

jobs and so What is the World For? Days.

Days of effort until the original poem

surfaces

through a search engine.

Dear,

To answer your text: it's <u>off</u> to be

returned. I saw a child in a mask with

another mask with another mask with

another mask. So

many straps. I

didn't think of you, I thought of me. What

drag—an after-event

that won't occur without the other—

no, more like popular radio: I'm survivin'.

Dear,

In the museum there is just one ash-man.

One is all I need to remember all the space

is not mine. My body is getting better

at being my own. I've been

breathing. Anyway

I can and won't erase your address

despite you

not not needing to erase

mine over there not any time

away, not needing

to say: Dear,

it's the lungs and it isn't the air,

it isn't count. I mean cut off the supply, I'm

FIRE

I need to say

I've been speaking

with a woman. I just met her.

She looks like

me. Behind her

3, 4, 5 copies of single books:

DEATH DRIVE,

WASTING AWAY,

JUST LIFE

She doesn't permit me to expend my

personal air until the room is empty; I don't

circle. I don't meet

myself.

I MAKE STUPID WORDS

I MAKE STUPID WORDS

I MAKE STUPID WORDS

I only know my Right Hand

performs interventions for my Left. All I

want my Left Hand to feel is that it is a

Good Hand.

No one need survive love;

love need survive no one;

my hands can come together now.   I invite

you in to the page:

GLORY BLOOM (ING) TON BE::RADHOW,
VIVRUSE::BE LOVE

I saw you in the Neighborhood Cooperative

buying meat, bread. You lined yourself

behind me,

perhaps I was not a woman you knew.

I was not a

woman when you knew me. I stare at your body against the magazines and I stare at your body. I pay for my Apostolic red wine and leave.

This is my wine's true name.

I was told you took a Bible to prison with you.

Because it is unfathomable

and because you could use it

for balancing exercises. I laughed when I

was told. I believed

nothing.

Nothing makes me think of you. The patient

ate STARCH, FAT, and a VEGETABLE a

day for 4 months and then the doctor

announced he is unqualified for further

duration of these

semantics.

      I said: a potato, butter, peas.

      A life inside

      a body was formed. I used my

already open eyes

to take up subjects and

consume them.   You told me I

reminded you of your mother

What did the rope remind you of?

Children.

Emptied sack.

I don't know. The silence that is actually an answer.

Children. Children. Children.

I was made to believe

everything, and here in the center

of December I bought a bottle of wine in the

Neighborhood Cooperative

and I can't turn

I can't turn

and tell you its name. It means

never ordering your emotions

until you are the crucible

not the contents.

TELL YOUR TRUE NATURE

TELL YOUR TRUE NATURE

TELL YOUR TRUE NATURE

I enter an online chat community. Strangers

are threaded by violence & you. One

suggests you be burned. I pat my arms.

At the stake.

I look around the room at the objects you suggested
I acquire to remind myself I exist: A white calla lily,
a small cold marble fox.

My hands begin to rub until friction. I stand

on one foot and feel

always either way without

myself.

Your associate at Mental Health &

Associates wears Coco

Mademoiselle and I am still wearing No. 5.

We meet in the middle

of the duration. You will never be recovered,

you knew her 20 years.

I say the word atonement.

I 25, 6 years a patient say: Excoriation

is only a mistake if you believe

in a future.   I stretch and smell

amber.

I was taught here to make a body for the

future.

I open up my laptop

and write against

history===I update

the browser, I keep shopping. I open to

The Guardian, to Forever 21, to Netflix. I

buy nothing most days but I do

some days. I'm here. I think of if there is

anywhere my body

my whole thing

can't go now, I think of the fire

wall, I think of you. It

was only one image

. I laugh. It was you

made me believe

evil too illegible

to exist.

HOLY WATER

HOLY MARBLE

HOLY GOD

HOLY WATER

HOLY MARBLE

HOLY MONSTER

WATER

I think I was raised by tree branches.

Things that

lifted me and swang back into space as

stepped off. This holiday,

I stay in R & S's empty house

where first I align all the gold pumps and in

one of the pump's toes

I find the foil pop of a champagne cork.

Other items:

a pink foam roller, a body-length

mirror I stack on four reference books

also THE YEAR OF DREAMING

DANGEROUSLY. I brought the last.

I put this at the end of the bed and now I see

myself upon awake. Have you ever

been abandoned? Have you ever been a

boat? Have you ever

been a thirsty bottle? Have you ever got so

good you became the

basin and had to ask: not where's the sky,

but also

why?

I expected this time

to come.

I have been so

satisfied. If you lived in this house and

observed plates of good food

are composed first of ordered lists: flour,

soda, herb, fat, you also would

trust a list. I have come here at the end of

the ordered

year. From Philadelphia,

from New Orleans,

from Atlanta,

text wakes me. We

are in our own zones. I hate my friends so

much.

I love my friends so much. It is like

need. Outside

an establishment

titled The Mill I see a taxi parked on the

sidewalk like an ambulance

in emergency. It is 11:00 am

on a Monday. It is break

and hard to make work like how poems

won't work,

how my mother won't work.

Have you ever tried to understand an element which wants nothing in exchange?

All the public pools

are emptied all across the nation. I try to

reach out without amplification and <u>I do</u>. I

Hotwire search a beach and the internet's

electronic calendars are covered

red letters and $$$. This house contains

more mirrors

than clocks.

My   m o the r

I sn't   in vited

to   this poem like

she isn't invited to

my dreams. Then I order these worlds. I'm going

t o   wake   up.

I don't know what time: at the Social Club

I announced I'm a child in my church. I saw a blonde

woman in a

bikini baptized in a Jacuzzi, she wore

an air-brushed unicorn cover-up. I don't

know how to know I am old.

I peeked

at my mother's dream journal last year: still

the dream the old thing crosses the threshold,

empties

me.

LET THE LINES MEET; ANEW THE LEAVES

ÆTHER

*

If no other <u>bodies</u>

*

Grant me a pistol

*

To fashion a billionth star.

*

If no other bodies

*

,no hands, hot pistols not forward

*

,Down. Earthward. Make earth

*

Smell of velocity, blow

*

The white away fffrom

*

My skull.

*

No hands.

*

In the middle, mouth

*

Tastes of stomach, iron, energy's ring.

*

That is why?

*

I keep my hands above my heart

*

And hear my blood

*

Rush.

      * *

If no other <u>ghosts</u>
    *   ***

Grant me a pistol
 *   * * ***

To fashion a second star.

C

O

S

M

O

L

O

G

Y

If I have to love
the flowers
at lowest allow myself to love

the crazed ones, the violent ones.

I want to eat the wild bluebell and die, I

mean to the botanists give shaped dust.

To the archivist give good record, give

the event in illumination. I have to press

against some weird dirt, some

clippings,

cuts. If I were a flower, I wouldn't

bleed

either, only eat. It is the nature of the sun

to offer without acknowledgement of receipt.

Archivist, imagine the menu of the banquet of

the light.

Archivist, imagine the oak upon which the sap

did corrupt.

Would that be noted? What about wax in its ulterior

state in between the bees' bearded

knuckles

bent not on becoming the vessel the wick can within

be contained; in fact not even an accessory to fire.

Archivist,

          ima

   River-backed the ghosts board the arkhe and
forget
          gine
       themselves! Eat over-
       stuffed limes lopped-over with
          the
       rum.

          menu

               No, I agree: Nostalgia
          isn't all it used to be.

Is anyone present possessed of any right questions?

The nature of the future is to never ask, to only
be asked after as the nature of the past is to never
be known, to love elision. To the senator give the surface

space under the eclipse, give the lowest layer
f the grave and from the juice of the green thing there grows:

the law of this garden,
the law of this garden,
the law of this garden,

Senator, love the last layer of the palimpsest.
Senator, love the original utter, the primary pollen, possessed,

of recipes received out of seeds begot not out of earth-plans.
Perhaps anyone is ready to write it? Possessed,

erhaps we are we confident animals in an ellipses?

p

How heavy lies the Samaritan
in the Angel's arms? Not as in an open
two breezes meeting from two
uncountried zones, but as to why
                              light
                              bounces
                              and wind
                              burns.

Frisk your own nature most ardently, adorn
your edges with blood-bruises.   Break with the broken
stalk.   At the last lush line
of the garden a woman kneels.   Kneeler,
was a walker; was planter; was lover.

                                        At

the last lush line of the garden
is an eater in a garden menued of rich
blonde-pineapple, tourmaline-strawberry, mushroom like
many dampened bells.

eat eat eat eat

If you don't reach the cosmos,
it isn't the end of the graph.

                                                        I

                                                        m

                                                        e

                                                        a

                                                        n

                                                        :

eat
at eat eat eat
eat eat
at eat eat eat
eat eat eat eat
eat eat eat eat
at eat eat eat
eat eat eat eat eat
at eat eat eat eat
eat eat
it eat eat eat

at eat eat eat eat
at eat eat eat eat
at eat eat eat eat eat
eat eat eat
eat eat eat eat
eat eat eat
eat eat
at eat eat eat
at eat eat eat
eat eat eat eat
eat eat eat eat
eat eat
eat eat eat eat eat
at eat eat eat
eat eat eat eat
at eat eat eat
at eat eat eat
eat eat eat eat eat
at eat eat   eat
at eat
at eat eat eat   eat
eat eat
at eat eat eat
at eat eat eat
at eat eat eat eat
at eat eat eat
at eat eat eat eat
at eat eat eat eat
eat eat eat eat eat
at eat eat eat
at eat eat eat
eat eat eat eat
at eat eat eat
at eat eat eat
at eat eat eat
at eat eat eat
eat eat eat eat eat eat
at eat eat eat
at eat eat eat
at eat eat eat
at eat   eat
at eat eat eat   eat
eat eat eat   eat
at eat eat eat eat
eat eat eat eat
at eat eat eat eat eat eat
at eat eat eat eat eat
at eat eat eat eat eat

i
f

y
o
u

h
a
v
e

n
e
v
e
r

h
e
a
r
d
,

y
o
u

d
o
n
,
t

k
n
o

w

h
o
w

t
o

l
i
s
t
e
n

n
o
,

i

m
e
a
n
:

i
f

y
o
u
'
v
e

n
e
v
e
r

e
a
t
e
n
,

y
o
u

.

d
o
n
,
t

k
n
o
w

h
o
w

t
o

b

e

h
u
n
g
r
y
.

Over-burdened, the Administrator's Assistant
is unsurprised Fidelorita is too thin, writes
codes for excess of ungoverned apple; accepts
not every author alive can walk within the orchard
but anyway checks again his collar for neon
lipstick, imprint—
the binary fatted valentine.

Hyper-articulated in the neo-filed garden under evenly
manicured cosmos, coin-cut constellation, I even want
to control my own limerence; I only
want to feel

what hands I feel. Even in the hour no other faces
account for my face, I find I cannot touch
my own fingertip. Even in the story of the map
of surface and suppression;

stomach and mouth; breakage and circuit; utter and occult;
I find in this construction I can only remain composition.
I cannot be talked out. Of all the offering I must not select
architect, cartographer, or even archivist. I,

in an ordered garden, a woman who often desires unachievable
disaster, must now desire dirt—mouthfuls, on my knees.
An animal who can leave a world must live in one.

A flood building in the body
A flood building in the body
A flood building in the body
A flood building in the body
A flood building in the body
A flood building in the body
A flood building in the body
A flood building in the body
A flood building in the body
A flood building in the body
A flood building in the body
A flood building in the body
A flood building in the body
A flood building in the body

Exit-less and riotous, everything on the arkhe

is afflicted of bluebell breath and heartburn; now
that the fence posts are in the wells emptied for fence
posts, a rumor that rebirth feels like death

by lack of potassium, a birth off the tongue;
blood and urine from unknown origins;
an invented language in the ear.

A flood building in the body,
A flood building in the body,
A flood building in the body.

The body *in this garden*,
the body-
build
ing.

GIVE

THE

EVENT-

IN

ILLUMINATION

의
ᄬ
ħ

ℱ

fluxed

DEMIURGE

As if a blueprint of author's imagined
Garden could begin without the 28 leathern paws
Of 7 unassigned dogs halting, holding
Their howls at the edge. If you draw me a map
I won't find you. This poem is for the cartographer
Offering an alternate arcadia, I mean, a third
Arcana. I mean I believe in spoil, wineskins
Accelerating unlit wars, ending ends. As if this poem
Isn't populated with obese angels and outsized
Stars, muzzled strong-men. But this poem is also
For a black smart phone screen, not networked
Or worked and inelegant without intelligence,
Molly-mirror unreflective of the unshiny other's
Intent, only an idea in abstraction upon lack
Of electrification. This poem is clearly for myself
Alone. My mother may have wrapped me in
A cloud. Because of this arrangement, I have
Insisted on some theories regarding ash and hair.
Instead, I ask myself if I mean vapor and ocean,
Air. I got good at this somewhere and now I need
To get deskilled, I am now only a spouse
To my true nature, a digger of foundation, fence
Posts. True. I have stayed here long enough to
Achieve, and now my arms are the arms of evident
Strength. I want to be the one in the kitchen,
Inhaling mint, wetted basil, the artifacts of exposed
Hearth. Upon first encounter, sugar
Was qualified as honey without bees. This seems to
Suggest that strength
–for a Cashiered Soldier or Bad Poet–
Is only intention without integrity. Howls

Echo in the uncharted empty even if the animals are
Not near; the nature of the canyon
Is to act and act again,
Reverberation. I mean to admit I remain
In the self-styled wild
Not out of an attitude of endurance
But in avoidance of the ultra
Charted zone, the solid city
Structured and clay-hardened.
Upon identification of the subject,
I collapse. Just as I cannot kiss the counter,
I cannot, cannot caress the fur of the domestic-dog
As if I cannot accept
The rope
That made the animal so, can only
Accept a cloud cannot be contained
Or rent

SCAPE

12 hounds assembled in the hard-scaped square &
I arrange my language in a series
of echoes, in a pathetic's effort made
my back available to none.............
...........Burden, answer your mail
encounter your ballot and awaken
to the skull's mis-pruned root scheme..............
Endure the dogs, do not swallow the vinegar,
do not swallow the gall, do not forget
yourself. 12 hounds assembled in the hardscaped
square &
I swallowed myself I could count everybone
I let them see everybone.
Bonebasket, hurry be a
being before the whip learns of the election.
Be before the post arrives and announces
through an advanced system of formal
pressure all bones are now broken, all bones
are now just unrhymed ideas............
Write a ~~poem~~ philosophy of your ribs,
there's nothing in the middle. Burden,
be a beggar—I mean uproot an unfair rose it is
always a rose. 12 hounds assembled in the hardscaped
square &
I drew the long handled knife out of my
back, out from under
my reed-hair. It had been there since before
&
Deus!
Filius!
Spiritus Sanctus!
I exited, unincorporated, unbound, still composed of
air.

composed of air. still composed of air. still composed
 of air. still composed of air. still composed of air.
still composed of air. still composed of air. still composed
of air. still composed of air. still composed of air.
composed of air. still composed of air. still composed
 of air. still composed of air. still composed of air.
still composed of air. still composed of air. still composed
of air. still composed of air. still composed of air.
composed of air. still composed of air. still composed
 of air. still composed of air. still composed of air.
still composed of air. still composed of air. still composed
of air. still composed of air. still composed of air.
composed of air. still composed of air. still composed
 of air. still composed of air. still composed of air.
still composed of air. still composed of air. still composed
of air. still composed of air. still composed of air.
composed of air. still composed of air. still composed
 of air. still composed of air. still composed of air.
still composed of air. still composed of air. still composed
of air. still composed of air. still composed

EX NIHILO

…every authentic poetic project is directed toward knowledge, just as every authentic act of philosophy is always directed toward joy.///Giorgio Agamben

Of course, Chaos
is not virtually nude, canola oiled,
genitals ensconced in an elect carcass.

Chaos
is the hypoglycemic girl-guide who contains
all the keys
all the keys to
all the city's access and
all the keys are sugar.
Chaos cannot contain
the complaints—
she admits there are no doors,
yawns, does not unzip, faints.

First I lick her keys into pens and knives and become a poet. Second I develop desire thus desire the development of doors but I have only pens and knives and so I poet hunger. Third I tire of poetry without anything to eat and eat my pens. Fourth I unzip Chaos out of each hunger and desire and after I again become a poet, so with my knife, I write. Fifth Chaos awakens and I reveal my writings written in blood.

Of course, nothing
in nature
causes Chaos to care
about poems.
Chaos won't button her own

khaki blouse, won't restrain
her recombinant bounce.
I enrage her
realm: It is all mirrors, in them all
myself asking the image of myself: Why
am I an animal that wants? I mean
what sort of pearl ravishes its shell
simply to be less raw, or
rather, are there any organs I possess
I would not traffic to travel farther out of the
organ of my own
skin? I am unincorporated
as concerns the limits of my own
living corpse—I can't
copulate with enough identical entities
to recognize myself at the other border-river's reflecting
space.
Again and again I recall instead an image from the
other shore:
Not of my mother.
No—of you,

you my friend

allowing me to envision my mother
and then envision myself
not like water but like light,
absorbing then exiting,
unafraid of an ending source.
Again and again in the easy access of the memory of
your listen, I am able to imagine
my mother in this way:
In Love,
amazing because a thing I never knew.
Of course, I knew you.

You were my Worth.
And to see you seeing your capacity
for potential capsize
all other options, to see you see yourself in the arms
of
the other
and out-living all
understood joy. This alters the identified arenas;
creates the livable unknown, concedes the lover may
never
be known,
allows me to let me
kiss open Chaos
and bloodless, be
the creatured
rising
          caring

FIDELITORIA, UNINC.

Once the air insects and lambs were placed

proportionally to their out-fittings, a 2nd
wave of chlorination was already in effect. One new
world can take
awhile.

First, the goat dug for fence post. Genuinely,
Novitiate, the word once forever
signifies messianic time. Last,
lightning altered its earth-object and consigned
the sky long-lasting debt,
over-drawn energy
and unavailable offer,
excepting glow:
nighttime hourglass, liquid map.

What were we
after anyway,
if not to only arrive
in the original case, in authentic carapace or wool or exo-
skeleton?
Some principalities have Kings
who can't lathe their capes b/c
uprising is imminent, imagine.
Imagine the breech baby Currency, appellate
for his first-born blathery Sister, River:
slattern and in exceptional eras,
salvadora doing the twist,

willing
willing
willing
to turn
in on herself
and flow against her own nature.
//////////////////
Some men never move themselves.

Novitiate, I've often allowed them access.
//////////////////
Imagine the King of the Principality of a Turned
River-Town.

Now,
imagine lightning first,
fence post last.

In exceptional areas
flood is the apparatus of achieved
intimacy with the celestial dome.
You only have to get a little closer
to be closer. Like Monies,
the eternal mother
—close & far close & far close & far—
must have named herself after
herself and also her eternal imprint
of her hieroglyphs:
like her mouth-feel, her name
means
baby-monitor,
means
I'm warning You of the White Swan Bachelorette

<u>Party</u>
means
<u>No Man Needs that Much Cash-in-Pocket.</u>
////////////////
How many mornings do you awake and ask to be
unafraid of the o t h e r - s i d e?
////////////////
This citizenry possessed of stars
and no fences
does not draw
constellations.
They don't circle-up and sing upon encounter of
empty
space. Once,
flight was thought to be the effort of every feather,
each fine-oiled device a muscled aerial in itself
until it was acknowledged
not only birds but bats, fish of the order Belinoformes,
aphids, wasps, a lot
of living creatures
also even balloon, arrow
could aircraft
unaided by visible support from any other surface.
////////////////
Novitiate, I am most afraid of loving the other incorrectly.

Novitiate, I am most afraid of offering no inner buoyancy.

Novitiate, I am most afraid of being asked what I want.
////////////////
Do you want to build your world with one orient?
A moon.
A mother.

About surface/space/ $$$:
heavenly phenomena
—stars, aurora, comets, clouds and airglow—
these objects historically unhindered
upon suppression of the central light source,
are bad counters
are excellence
&
are up there
serving no one

FIDELORITA

Fidelorita was counting the nests of the birds
In the birches and beeches, Fidelorita
Could not keep count, could not believe
At the bottom, there was anything. Fidelorita
Has a father. Of course.
Fidelorita lives on a Plant.
Fidelorita had a mother. Fidelorita
Feels like I feel.
As if she is a Fairy
Tale feeling.

Her hands have never built a fence/ or rather if you ask
her to essay on freedom she will write a riddle regarding
etymology and root systems.

Her hair has never been
Cut, its ends are filthy, glutted
With gross honey, aglow with synthetic milk,
Appraisable with the pixilated saffron
Of Fidelitoria. Her mother
Was a tabloid/an alien
Ation. Her mother was why Fidelorita looked
Upward, expectant, was herself a fixed fortune for a
Fluxed kingdom. A synonym for Reason is Sanity. Do
You yourself always know what to do
With you hands?

Bird-bait, eco-flirt
Ation. Grow, growing, grown. Fidelorita's
Father's name is King Cause his blood is made of

Ink, of
Gossip. No one needs a newspaper
In Fidelitoria but everyone needs rope.

Accept it, as fast as you can.
Aging hour,
Decrepit clock,
Heat-ravaged organs.
Everyone is opposite
Fidelorita in Fidelitoria.

Fidelorita finds fresh rope but can think of
Nothing
To do with rope,
Has no ideas to tie herself to

[SUBJECT] DESIRE

Imagine a composition

almost only of bones—

an architecture of incomplete

energy, upholding. When the contemporary-animal

said survive

yourself, she meant endure

yourself. An energy rattling

on, ulna, fibula

meta

tarsals

banging, bang against a skin-box. Rap.

Rap. So dry

her marrow, her only

fatness is all the give giving way,

porous elements

closing shut, nerves shutting off

&

emptying access to senses. Trigeminal

area dead. She only meant

endure yourself even if you are called

upon to forget

your body, to breathe through

recessed reeds. If worried about death, try to really

die.

Rap. Rap.

Fidelorita, myself must be excessive

to remain. Against the wall accounts cannot be

settled. The desk

must be moved

to the center

of the office

& even office must become

another order.

ALWAYS
ORDER
ALWAYS
ORDE
R
ALWA
YS
ORDER

Please accept that affect of armature

[She also holds suspect the unriven logic of

lightning, or ice.

She also only trusts the starving animal holding still,

call her bear.]

Name one thing

unforged through pressure. [She admits she loves

her trappings:

stocking, wire, wrap, mammalian muff.]

Permission-seeking a magic granting

gesture, Fidelitorita often asks

for others. So if she may

proceed to describe the case

overstuffed with glass goblets, globules, globes

of crystal

before explaining glass or any world once forged is

only

an element fit

for breakage

in its next incarnation. [You will know animality,

reader,

by its lack of transience

flesh among flesh

an etymology of no exchange; carnation colored the

color of skin.

No, not that.

Rather, the glass encased glass holds

many orbs of emptiness appearing otherwise.

Vague schematic of grandeur,

does every jewel diamond to the eye that apprehends

no spectrum—

diamond/dark diamond.] Or,

how does one know a luster upon approach? What

era indicates a linger? But

yes, this case

unable to delimit its contents,

its uncharitable anti-archive of shimmers

cast. Greened magenta clear unmagnifiable motion,

mid-sip of medicinal airs,

Fidelorita will state

her true

meaning: is she the forged or the forger, & if

slips a long bone from left arm with right

& fragments all the obtrusive

gems—what

stands to bear then? You'll

know her by the upright

order of her easy approach.

Attempt to envision a life

free of shelves, unfastened to others

figurines, language did you do this disambiguation?—

Others

mimetic impulses, mascara corset fatted mouth, all

was meant. Once bear had

two mentors & one said never write of rabbits

if what you mean is

glory unto death, all

you have is running & endurance, write instead of

silver shot fur & the other

mentor said write only of rabbits, if

you ever bite down you

die regardless.

Anyway, it only takes two points to make a line,

two joints to join a bone to skeleton.

Also attacks come direct,

unlike life lived in the open field. She does wish

she could demand you

know her

by her defenseless posture;

her denuded feet

once cut through the callus

& compressed to acknowledge no wealth

in compression. Counterfeit, what was the wild to a

burden like Fidelorita?

Did she eat

anything?

Many times

her mouth was full

of light. Ash &

operable steam which

informed on the organized rays; ordered

rain. Fidelorita did not belong

there

but she stayed.

<u>DIS</u>

<u>ORDER</u>

<u>DI   SORDER</u>

<u>DISORD</u>

<u>ER</u>

Copy synonymous with nothing, the brunt

ultralanguage of exact diction exited. Rough

tongue, abandoned by a mute monster. Rough

tongue, birthed on junk-words, you'll know her

by her exit.

She'll be the

light one

loping out of a body,

into exactly another body

APOLOGIST

And if there are also flowers in hell

There are also flowers in here; can I qualify
That? I mean, is there a quality to that
Which can only be gotten at if I admit my limit
Is tempered only by my access to others? I am
An animal who needs to beg.
I need
To know
What my bones are for: my knees, my knuckles,
The long stretch of skin along my back I never
Encounter. If my hands are open they are not
Closed. Ask the architect about the gate
To receive
An answer on the hinge.

The deer has been in the impasse since the Hunter
left. Ask

The artist about the body
To receive an answer on the gate. An interlude
Is not an excuse, for
Example it is a pleasure to experience
Another's weight allowing a second access to my
Own burden,
As when you cover me so completely I am
Allowed experimental cartography;
For a stretch our skin is ours and
Still I do not encounter myself. I need
To walk through the gate
Forever and you tell I was talking in my sleep

In your dream. I am a woman who needs
To see her own back. Ask the poet
A question.

Is the face the most sacred or the most secular
Object on the earth?

In the other's hands in the open
It is neither, but in the alien's hands in the open
It is both. Again, I cite the diction when at
Outskirts is the syntax. Against
Myself I mean to demand encounter of the
Frame, not the contents; not the face
But the open hand.

The deer has been in the impasse since the Hunter
left. Ask

The listener a question and meet your own
Masks; other halves in abrupt, unanticipated
Echo. Not the affixed inner, the elected outer
As the moon in cycle
Except exception is created
For the disnature of earthshine; over-lit arenas
Of rock in the planet's dark limb. I
Didn't intend to encounter you. Hunter,

I asked the wrong questions. Hunter,
Why did you leave me with this dotted hide,
Softness

SOFT

Sort of error. My real hair, unhinged
from my head. Was I a blonde-girl
anymore or an experimental light, a
way for others to see through water,
ashes? I have already said what I am afraid
of. Yonder. I ask my father on the other
end about procession, peaceful
parting: Candie, keep yourself and give
your things. He means give up, give
way. Keep falling from windows
in order to assure the greatness of your
own height, if only to be the wreck
of your own pure lightness. Only
on a second story hotel balcony, bonds
can be broken with the world one
can come to skim, to see as surface. Chlorinated,
incalculable current unbearable without
tallied reflections. Stop. In the rented
room's mirror, the face I deserve and under-
neath, another atmosphere I have never
endured: I doubt it is oceanic, operable
by infallible salts or expanse of warm blues,
cool blues. An indigo, a lapis, a lazuli. Instead
I suspect a smallness
No—a clarity
No—a clarity
No—a clarity,
A cross at a crossing,
A dryness delivering, upending as does specifically
dirt in demand of a grave. Just
a thin yield, as earth under blade, giving

to pressure within freeze, shale.
I know the odd dumb organ breaks
beneath my breasts, never showing
and only even aware of itself because of the
occasioned hand pushing back my hair to comment
I can hear your
self. Have I already said
what I am afraid of; I have already
tried to fuse this, this
bare flicker
nude synapse

FUCK OFF

Bravery was nothing, call it the escaped whelp.
Call it the emotion with no memory & no count, no
rhythm and therefore no record worth repetition
for the keeper's account. Bravery was nothing
but the dumbest animal's ability to stand and stand
and stand alone in the pasture past the time
others felt en masse.   I would not think
through. In
order to allow for every hoof you have to harm
the hard-packed earth, I stood still. I am I am
monster
of endurance for you, it happened while I was
holding
my heart in a bag by the bag I keep my stomach in;
I told you I don't need to eat—you eat. I'm admiring
you, your
babied teeth and curated crawl. You
ravenous wolf, you whip. I want to be a bride's
maid all my life in your eternal train only because
you
promised to marry
everything; only
because I'm the bitch
& you're the doggess I did it for.
Hound-girl, would I have come to believe there was
light
worth love without your howl? I mean
to know an unshatterable
slant, resilient
strain.
Of all the concrete covering the earth,

also all the low pools of dim dark glow,
also in the end even I when alone
ended in the street, with another,
explaining I counted on you to count myself and
having lost
you, I was only
nothing.
I need two
to know I was
one.
I needed the forgery
to know I was unforged
creation.

THE FANTASMATIC PROJECTION

Love's crime impacted the stabled
Population's plans for masking
Tape, gauze, electronic records. Even
Animals who ranged most wild
Learned to nurture their farewells.
Scavengers began to feed others first, thus
Outmoded dictions were addressed.
Hunt → banquet.
Prey → acquaintance.
[I was a woman who wondered why
We did not murder the old words.]
I could chant about the amount of language
Taken to resurrect & write, but
            you know.

Expect an animal, a megafaun, too easy with the exclamative
marker. Expect an instant, a megafauna, that holds the non-
space, doesn't need your sexy carcass.

Criminal, the supermarket observation screen freezes
You hoarding hothouse African roses, lavender nail
Lacquer, chocolate, rubbers, arrows, gin.
Criminal, stay stafe.
Criminal, I see you load yourself and I think on the
Image of the soldier,
Gun strapped to his operating hand –
Wound thrice
With a critically misused bandage.

Criminal, it was a moment of puncture made me

Make marks on the page. I named this crime

Out-of-the-Law and so now
I see the citizenry in merciless faith imagine
I will know enough unclassifiable joy
After enough
Returns.

THERE IS NO THIRD POSITION

Obsessed with the image
Of the cashiered soldier:
Epaulettes, insignia, every gold
Button burst and with the blade of a sharper blade,
The blade of the red velvet soldier's blade
Razed, I become a woman
Who wonders: what does it mean to be
One who cannot even
Sell yourself? It can take a long time
To produce that worth giving away, I mean a ghost
Is free but one must know death to experience such
Illumination.

Attic, cement room,
Open the windows at any cost
In a city with a drunken city planner
Balls, a bottle in a cello, another fat gold fox
In a city with a drunken city planner
A museum becomes careless
With color and an exhibit on flowers is curated
So the citizenry appears
In a city with a drunken city planner
Overlapping tiles creating under-lapping
Spaces called out at hundreds
Of angles, at least a
Hundred and a hundred and hundred fifty-nine in the in
-Exact gorge
In a city with a drunken city planner

Obsessed with the image
Of the cashiered soldier:

I asked myself
The wrong questions in order
To ask what the soldier wore
After. I asked about the event and heard
The word
Ash, mask, rash, and decision infected in
The word:
Ask. I asked if there were any other garments on
Earth which would endure all weather, an un
Aleatory outfitting of a person all alone. I ask because
I love
My own
Personal silk. Here is a list of that
Which others who identify with me have told me are
Fun and Easy:
Dating, sleeping, eating, easing
Out of the clearing into the thicket, ness.
Only one space I know
Of converts from a space for confession
Into a space for crying, and back again and
Again. I especially appreciate the garment in which I am
cloaked so splendidly I
Am unavailable to even I, I
Am a woman who can make this occur.
It is often
All I've got.
Obsessed with the image
Of the cashiered soldier:
I remove my own
Outfitting, cough up any vestigial maps,
Vestal lighters, unauthorized gloss,
Improperly packaged petrol.
Every item I absconded from what I thought the last

Stable stop on earth, and I go then.

In a city with a drunken city planner
Bedroom, library
Enters sheets and parts them at any cost
Baby, bottle, green lighting on the dry dark day
In a city with a drunken city planner
A soldier strips and stands beside her soldier-skin
With love shaped like a box beside another box
Another ensign O, X
Over all the city standard sidewalks awash with chalk
Gold Green Acid Indigo no one's curated colors
In a city with a drunken city planner
An event is to stand by one's self standing by one's
Self standing in the street
Unaligned

PSYCHOPOMP///CONVERSATION ARTIST

My car must stop nine times before the Recreation &
Wellness Center.
All I really believe is in the center
Of all other rings, an
Emptiness. A workshop
On Intuitive Eating is occurring, I
Am also. Modern physicians
Prescribe premeditated mindfulness
But even the sauna is not safe
For me. I am a waxen wicket. I have
Illegible energy; I was once a poet
Now I am a Burden. I mean I cannot not
Restart. In the locker
Room, there are no keys,
Only those with quarters.
Is it possible
A drift like me expects nothing
From another?
I am often
Alone, expect to exceed farther
From any established eros, agape. 1000 miles
From my imagined garden.
All I really believe is act as if there
Is no center.
Often, I desire
A fence to float through,
An institution to respect.
Often I stretch and pleasure.
Often I keep
Repeating myself until I myself transfigure into
My own archival instance.
This one is my one act of artistry.
On the treadmill's loop

I become my own
Other and intuitively, I feel
I know what it must have been to be the last good
Militia-man,
A vault of chemicals even-stepping the squares
Asking all others for identification
Often asking also myself and honor-bound
To endure a self-set curfew.
Oh, yes.
In this expenditure, I feel
The foundation-fixed face I want
To want and have
Evacuating, sweating
As the aura of the second asserts,
Incomprehensible belief babbling
That she is composed
Of only words
And will be awake all night
And in any circlet of—obsidian, aluminum,
Inorganic—glass I will distinguish
This un-cored brain.
This matters.
This chatter does not fill
Hours, only
Cities, suggests
There is no inner
Petal, and if no bloom
Perhaps no
Paradiso, and perhaps if there is no
Center here, there is simply
No inferno

Anywhere

MONDAY

Thanks, &&&&&
for the poem I needed to read. I keep
expecting to stop and its always
tomorrow in my mouth. March
can be the coldest month because I want
to say Love has no memory
but I won't. Any morning, wake
to a bird who belongs in a burnishing
tree, an oriel, in honesty—I never
learned their names. I mean
thaw behavior in a rhythm country
can cause this kind of lack, this dearth
of courtesy.
This is my 30th spring.
This is my 30th spring.
This is my 30th spring.
In the ice I even have energy, what is water
to a woman like me; a technology
of transit, and not transience. Shine. Feathers
free the unbound, I oil
and plume. I insist on Monday
and it always is. A song
resounds exact in memory, an architecture
of lung, heart and other organ arranges
everything and what collisions to suggest
anything else except me. Sparrow,
direct to sleep almost
nothing is about me
except I am always
here. All
I can expect is to keep
arriving, apparently
nothing will depart. It appears
this is still

[IS]LAND

Into a yellowing spring. I now see
Eleven years into my adulthood
I am a woman who will empty herself
Of resistance upon encounter of light,
Of any color.
I do not hesitate to drive, or even walk,
In the direction of deep shades
Of zodiacal darkening. Of the hot
Pink electronic emptiness
Released in any neighbor's window.
What is worse is when

An area

Unexpectedly unlocks, whitens and blinds. I
Am resistant to open my own mail.
Unbound,
I like to live

Lightly, in love with loosed earth, unlimited
To dirt, demarcated not by roots or the limbs
Of other's trees, but by fallen leaves, the wash

Off graves. I know I sound like a little ghoul

Girl but too often I want to stand
At a platform, a sub
Way structure ajar into winter and not wish
For other
Seasons or times, of course I have lived all these
Years under and I am committed
To understanding the intent

Of animals with eyes not opened

Up all the way. Moles,
Little rock babies, unhaired
Fatty mammals don't differentiate between
Dream and day, do not invent a thing like

A curtain. What is furniture except another

Apparatus? A way to insist

On eating inside a human house? I
Try harder & I try higher to send sounds through

The tubes & tunnels
That access womanish words, I
Pull closed the shower door, I cover my nails beds

With lacquer and shine and in another
Effort at impossible peopling, I speak and sound like
ideas. Red, pink

Plastic carnations, photos, other fancy trash
Flooded out from the uppermost monuments
Fence the edges of the memory garden. Far

Away a flying thing rings itself with its own
Feathers, it takes hours and it takes hours and
It happens everyday and as I approach
The season

Of the extension of the light of the hours
I try also

To enter the circlet, to be not only surrounded

but touched.

DOES the INTERLOCUTOR NEED a GUN CHAMBER, a SATELLITE DISH?

Admit the interlocutor's mansion invoked desire:
a structure by which one
is served a menu from which one
selects and is served.
We mainlined on autumning cuts, beige
sheen, paisley, pine spheres, centaur
flesh. Our longings
serpentined
so quickly
we hailed them.
We reached
across one another's china, dipped
blousons in obscure sauces. Haste
becomes the base of being.
As if our language contained the grammar for
apology.
We considered our parents,
setting us up, or down.
At the interlocutor's mansion the elements were
other:
oil, marshmallow, hair, pages.
There was no quintessence, time was not everywhere.
At the axis of
reworks &
reworld &
reword me with an/other
I de-cored cannot even re/quest you admit
in the interlocutor's mansion
I was your dinner companion,
I may have only believed it was you.

Imagine I spilt salt
and refused to embarrass myself
with learned history, a refusal
to acknowledge anything
over, or against my shoulder. As if I was not made
of salt, as if I was made of need
for more
world crystals, tooth & tongue kissing in complexity.
I'm not sorry I can taste so much iron, or gold.

The interlocutor is dipped in guilt:
but his mansion is mere sequin, sandstone,
bushes burning with lavender, sage, amber, yarrow.
The Spirit Realm vomits to smell his Real Estate.
He is hot, here.

Once,
My father sang the chorus of a song from his youth
over the whole of a song from mine,
his voice slowed to speed of snow,
another abundant echo
I had not noticed.

MEDIUM

I don't know if this is the right place
To approach this. The light of the library
Aisle will not light until after I enter.
I am designed to endure ultra-dazzle or ultra-
Dark.
I am at the outset of my life,
I am a woman who desires aliens. Even
Though unable to identify the hand
Out of the over or under-bright
I want to
Believe the touch's un-believability
Is accounted for
By systems
Of belief.
Honestly, Alien, I offer myself in good faith. Who
Am I to quote any other author on earth?
I love you.
Already all my words are re-corded,
Strings bent and blown mid-note. I do
Not fuck off to any failure of vision, I & you
Are experiencing the same song in this
Open stack. I swear.
About the dark: my posture
Is only the uniform of the institution
And if this ink makes the paper
Worth less, then my position in the light
Implies all I have is my shadow and my other
Shadow.
But I'm here.
I mean, I desire the imprint of your eyes
In the ink dark
Where I am alien to myself
Where I now sense there is only one

Kind of currency.
I used to need another who would know
My name in heaven.
Alien, now I do not even know
What my name was yesterday
In the over-comforted bed clothes,
Quilted down pink
Upon pink, every organ
Of transmission in silent concert with
My mimetic self—
How can this now be recalled, my name did not wear
make-up at all—
Anyone had made a decision
About satin and a mirror which forced reflection on
Badiou:
Love is not a contract
Between two narcissists.
I could recall because I was alone
And could not see myself or any ripple,
Refurbished ripple, of myself. A sleep
Chamber produces a couple squared, squared
Kinds of experiences, experimental sentiments.
Lace edge, dying strain, French scene.
As a child I entered the hot space
Under the sheets
And called it Ocean and endured it until
I couldn't,
Until I couldn't feel enough
Oxygen. Untrue to say we only perceive the air
If we witness the air act upon an object. I sense
Your name, Alien, although I do not know it

&

Also, no here and also no heaven.

Only this layer,
And enough,
And another—

Acknowledgements

Thank you to the journals in which some of these poems originally appeared, including: *The Colorado Review, The Volta, The Atlas Review, Dusie, Prelude, Medium, SAND: Berlin's English Literary Journal, Deluge, Boaat, GlitterMOB, SPORK, La Vague, Ohio Edit, Fruita Pulp, Flag+Void, SET, Jerry* and *Inter|rupture.*

The sequence "Earth," "Air," "Fire," "Water," "Æther" was originally published as a chapbook by Grey Book Press as EARTH AIR FIRE WATER ÆTHER.

Appreciation

Thank you to Andrew Wilt and the team at 11:11 for giving this book a home and a place to shape shift into its final form. Thank you to Mike Corrao for all the energy devoted to the design of this book. Thank you to my teachers, especially Joseph Harrington, Joyelle McSweeney, Donna Stonecipher, and D.A. Powell. Finally, thank you to my friends who read and inspired many versions of this project: Amelia Bird, Meredith Blankinship, Jared Harvey, Rachel Milligan, Patrick Reed, and Sean Zhuraw.

CPSIA information can be obtained
at www.ICGtesting.com
Printed in the USA
LVHW070110140421
684383LV00033B/1786